TITLES IN THE KEEPING HEALTHY SERIES:

# • Personal Hygiene • Eating • Safety
# • Exercise • Relationships • Harmful Substances

© 2004 White-Thomson Publishing Ltd

Produced by White-Thomson Publishing Ltd
2/3 St Andrew's Place, Lewes, BN7 1UP

| | |
|---|---|
| Editor: | Elaine Fuoco-Lang |
| Consultant: | Chris Sculthorpe, East Sussex, Brighton & Hove Healthy School Scheme Co-ordinator |
| Inside design: | Joelle Wheelwright |
| Cover design: | Hodder Wayland |
| Photographs: | Robert Pickett |
| Proofreader: | Jane Colgan |
| Artwork: | Peter Bull |

Published in Great Britain in 2004 by Hodder Wayland, an imprint of Hodder Children's Books. Hodder Children's Books, a division of Hodder Headline Limited, 338 Euston Road, London, NW1 3BH.

British Library Cataloguing in Publication Data
Ballard, Carol
  Relationships. - (Keeping Healthy)
  1. Interpersonal relations - Juvenile literature
  I. Title
  158.2

ISBN 0 7502 4340 6

Printing and binding at C&C Hong Kong.

Acknowledgements.

The publishers would like to thank the following for their assistance with this book: the staff and children of Salmestone Primary School, Margate, Kent.

Picture acknowledgements:

Angela Hampton Family Picture Library 17 top, 18, 19 bottom, 29 top; Chris Fairclough 4; Ariel Skelley/CORBIS 7 bottom and 24, Tom & Dee Ann McCarthy/CORBIS 8, Jennine Woodcock/CORBIS 16, Randy Faris/CORBIS 20, Earl & Nazima Kowall/CORBIS 27 bottom; Hodder Wayland Picture Library 5 top, 17 bottom, 25 top, 27 top; Robert Pickett 5 bottom, 6, 7 top, 9, 10, 11, 12, 13, 14, 15, 19 top, 21, 22, 23, 25 bottom, 26, 29 bottom 31; WTPix 28.

The photographs in this book are of models who have granted their permission for their use in this title.

# Contents

# About relationships

Relationships are the many different ways in which we are linked to the people, animals and other things around us. The relationship between two people affects how they feel about each other and how they behave towards each other. The relationship can also affect how they feel about other people and their attitudes to other things around them.

Some relationships can be very close, such as the close bond many twins feel towards each other. Other relationships can be more distant, such as that between a child and a relative they rarely see or hear from.

▲ *Often siblings form strong bonds. Twins can have a special relationship.*

Our society is made up of relationships between all the people who live in it. We all contribute to our society, and the places in which we live, work and play are happier and more pleasant when we try to be polite and considerate to others.

Families are important because the framework of close relationships within a family can help to make us feel safe and secure. Friends are important because they also provide close relationships that we can enjoy and rely on.

▲ *Helping people older than yourself helps to contribute to a happy society.*

◄ *It is great to have a wide circle of friends. It is also nice to share your thoughts with a close friend that you can rely on.*

# What makes a family?

A family is a group of people who live together. Our families are important to us because they provide love, support, security and a feeling of belonging. Families can be made up of all sorts of different groupings of people.

Many families consist of a mother and father and their children. This was often seen as a standard sort of family and is frequently found in many older books and films. Now, more and more families are made up of different groupings.

## !?/ Fantastic Facts

In the nineteenth century in western countries, it was not uncommon for a husband and wife to have 20 children! This was partly because many children died when they were very young, and so the more babies you had, the more likely it was that at least one would live to be an adult.

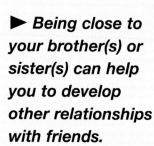

► *Being close to your brother(s) or sister(s) can help you to develop other relationships with friends.*

## Living with one parent

Many families are made up of a child or children and just one parent, either a mother or a father. Sometimes, the children may see their other parent, perhaps at weekends or holidays. Sometimes, they may never see them at all.

▶ *It feels good to have help and support from a parent.*

## New family members

Often, two families join together to make one new, larger family. Two parents may decide to live together with all their children.

## Extended family

Most people think of their family as being made up of more people than just those who live in their house. Aunts, uncles, cousins, grandparents are all part of our families too. In some communities, these relationships are very close.

▲ *A birthday party is enjoyable for the whole family.*

# Being part of a family

A family is happiest when each of the individual people in it is happy. This means that no one person can have things all their own way all the time. Each person has to think about the needs of all the others, rather than just selfishly thinking about themselves.

Often, two members of a family want different things and it is impossible for both to have what they want. For example, you may want to watch one television programme while somebody else wants to watch another. This needs a compromise, which means that both people have to give in a little bit. Perhaps one could watch their programme while the other is recorded, and swap it around next week? This is much better than arguing over it.

▲ *Enjoying activities together, like watching a sport, is fun for all the family.*

▲ *Trusting your brother or sister is a very important part of developing a friendship.*

We all expect the members of our families to love us, help us and support us. We expect to be able to trust them and rely on them, and we expect them to be honest and truthful with us. This only works if everybody in a family tries to do the same. If one person is selfish, dishonest or unreliable, then they cannot expect help and support from the others.

## Action Zone

A family works best when each person in it tries to help everybody else. Can you think of a way in which you could help each member of your family? Perhaps you could listen to a younger brother or sister read, or offer to play a game they choose. Could you make a special effort to be quiet while an elder brother or sister does their homework? Would your parents like some help to clear away after a meal? Perhaps you have some ideas of your own.

▶ *Helping with jobs around the house helps to build good relationships within a family.*

# Friends and friendships

There is a well-known saying – To have a friend, you need to be a friend, – but have you really thought about what it means? It is really just a way of saying that friendship is a two-way thing: if you want somebody to care about you and help you, then you have to be ready to care about them and help them too.

Do you like to be with a large group of people, perhaps playing with some one day and others the next? Or do you stick very closely to the same one or two people all the time? Perhaps you fall somewhere between the two, with one or two special friends and a bigger group who you are friendly with too. Each of these types of friendship is good, as long as you always think about how the others are feeling. Are they all happy? Is anybody feeling left out or let down? If so, can you do anything to help?

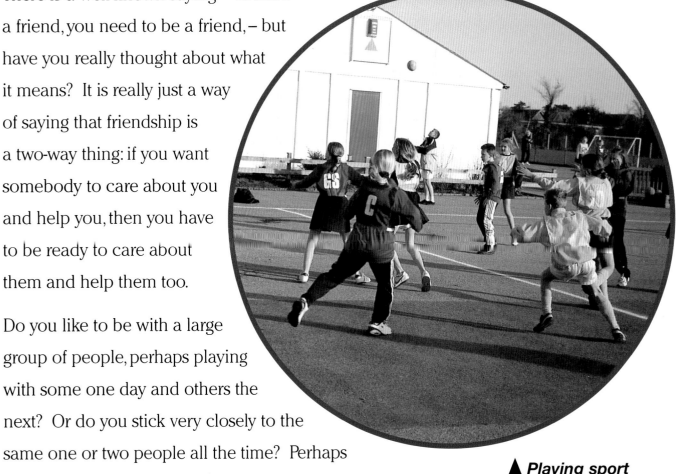

▲ *Playing sport is a great way to make friends.*

### New friends

Friendships can change as you grow up. Both you and your friends will grow and interests and attitudes change. These changes may make you even firmer friends or they may lead to new friendships being formed. This is nobody's fault, but it can cause a lot of unhappiness if someone sees their best friend becoming closer to somebody else. You can help to prevent this by making sure that you are as kind to your old friends as you are to your new friends.

▶ *Friends can enjoy many things together, like these ice-creams!*

 **Healthy Hints**

Are you a good friend? Look at this checklist.

Good friends:

- are kind and caring
- are fun to be with
- keep each other's secrets
- try to help each other
- are honest, loyal and reliable.

Would your friends give you a tick for each of these? If not, what could you do to be a better friend?

▲ *It can be fun to compete against your friends.*

# Joining in

Do you look forward to your breaks from lessons at school so that you can spend time with your friends? Most people do, and the free time spent playing games or chatting can be good fun. Can you imagine how unhappy you would feel if you had nobody to play with or talk to? Some children have very few friends, so they are often lonely and miserable.

▲ *Try not to leave somebody sitting miserably on their own. These girls could easily let the lonely girl join in their conversation.*

# Healthy Hints

If you feel lonely and left out a lot of the time, perhaps you could help yourself a little. Don't just stand and watch others playing or talking, go and ask if you can join in. People are often left out simply because the others do not know they want to join in! If they say no, don't argue or sulk, try to find another group to be with instead.

▲ *Joining in games helps us to make friends.*

There are lots of different reasons why some children are left out of activities. Children will stay away from anyone who is mean, spiteful or dishonest, and you may feel that people who behave like this do not deserve to have any friends. Often, though, there may be no real reason for someone to be left out. Rumours about somebody can start easily and people may hear them and believe them, without bothering to find out whether they are really true. It is always best to ignore rumours, and never to start them yourself, as they can upset other people.

▼ *A friendly welcome can make somebody feel happy and wanted.*

# Teams

When you talk about teams, many people just think of team sports like basketball and football. Teams are also important in many other things: your school is probably run by a team of teachers, and countries are run by teams of people that we call governments. For a team to work well, each person has to think about what is best for the whole team, rather than just for him or herself.

▼ *This ball game relies on the team members helping each other.*

Team members need to talk, listen and discuss things with each other, to let them know what is happening and what they need or expect them to do next. They need to co-operate too, to help each other make the most of every chance. Every team member needs to be able to trust and rely on all the other team members all the time. Team members need to encourage each other if they are trying to do something difficult, praise each other when something goes well, and be understanding and kind when something goes badly. Each team member needs to try to do their best all the time, so that the whole team will benefit.

▲ *A tug-of-war needs every team member to do their very best.*

# \!?/ Fantastic Facts

It is not only humans who work as a team, many animals do too. Some flocks of birds fly in a V pattern, and they all have to work together to maintain this pattern. The front bird has to work hard to navigate and lead the rest of the flock. When it tires, it gradually falls back into the pattern and another bird moves forwards to take its place. They all take it in turns to do the hard work of being leader, and then to have a rest.

► *Some birds, like these flamingos, work in a team.*

# Bullies and bullying

What are bullies and bullying? Basically, bullying is anything that one person does to another that makes them unhappy. A bully is anybody who bullies somebody else.

Physically hurting somebody on purpose is bullying. Pushing, tripping, kicking, punching, pulling hair – all of these would hurt somebody and are examples of things that a bully may do.

People can be bullied emotionally as well as physically. Leaving somebody out all the time, whispering behind their back, spreading rumours, spiteful teasing and telling tales are all examples of emotional bullying.

▲ *Ganging up on someone isn't very nice and you wouldn't want to be the person being picked upon.*

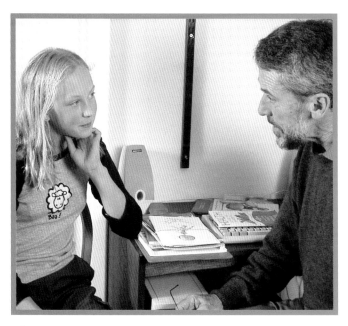

▲ *Being bullied can be very upsetting, but talking to an adult can often help to sort out the problem.*

Bullies are often helped by other people. Some help the bully and encourage him or her to carry on. Some copy the bully's actions. Most just stand and watch what is happening without doing anything about it. If the onlookers decided to defend the victim or to get adult help, the bullying would soon stop. If you're ever in this situation, don't just stand there – do something! Do think about your own safety first, though. Never put yourself in danger, ask an adult to help instead.

# Healthy Hints

If you think or know somebody is being bullied you should:

● Tell an adult you can trust, such as a parent or teacher. Don't worry, you are not telling tales, you are helping somebody who cannot help themselves.

● Support the victim as much as you can. Try to make sure they are not on their own when the bully is around.

● Encourage the victim to talk to an adult about the bullying.

▲ *If you feel threatened, ask an adult for help.*

# Gangs

A gang is a group of people who spend their time together. They may not mean any harm, but some gangs do often upset other people. Some gangs are just a collection of friends, but others are more formal and may have special rules, passwords and secret signs. Gang members often have

▲ *It is good to have a group of friends who you can rely on.*

the same likes and dislikes as each other. They may listen to the same music, read the same magazines, wear the same clothes and enjoy the same activities.

Gangs can often act as bullies. A group of people all picking on one or two others can cause a lot of upset and hurt. Each individual gang member may only say or do one thing, but the whole lot together can be very distressing for the victim.

When people are in a gang, they often do things that they would never do on their own.

One person might start something that then gets taken a bit further by somebody else, and so on, until the situation gets completely out of hand. It might seem fine at the time, but the individual gang members may feel very embarrassed and ashamed later because, together with the rest of the gang, they have harmed another person or people – something they would not do on their own.

▲ *Being bullied can be very upsetting.*

 # Healthy Hints

It makes sense not to get involved with a gang. If you have a group of friends who all share many of the same likes and interests, that's fine but make sure your group does not hurt anybody else, even accidentally. Try not to have secret rules as these can lead to a lot of trouble.

▶ *Belonging to a gang who pick on others is not a good way to develop strong relationships.*

# Peer pressure

Your peers are all the children around you of the same age as you. This includes the children in your class, in sports teams you play for and in clubs that you might belong to. Peer pressure means the ways in which you feel you have to behave because of what the other children around you might say or might think.

Peer pressure can have a positive influence. For example, if everybody in your class is learning their spellings for a test, you will probably feel that you should do the same.

▲ *Always be comfortable with how you act. Even in front of your peers you shouldn't feel you have to do anything you don't want to do.*

# \?/ Fantastic Facts

Some companies rely on peer pressure to help them sell their product. If they can make something that is easy to identify, such as a top with a special logo, everybody in your peer group can see if you have that top. If the rest of your group has it, you're probably going to want it too, just to be the same, so the company makes even more money!

► *Do all your friends like to wear the same clothes?*

Peer pressure can also be harmful and cause a lot of unhappiness. If everybody around you wants to do something, it can be very difficult not to join in. You should always try to do what you know is right and sensible, however hard the others try to persuade you to follow their lead. Never let others persuade you to do something you know to be wrong or dangerous. If there is a real problem, make sure you tell an adult about it.

▼ *Talk to an adult if you are being pressured to do something you are not happy about.*

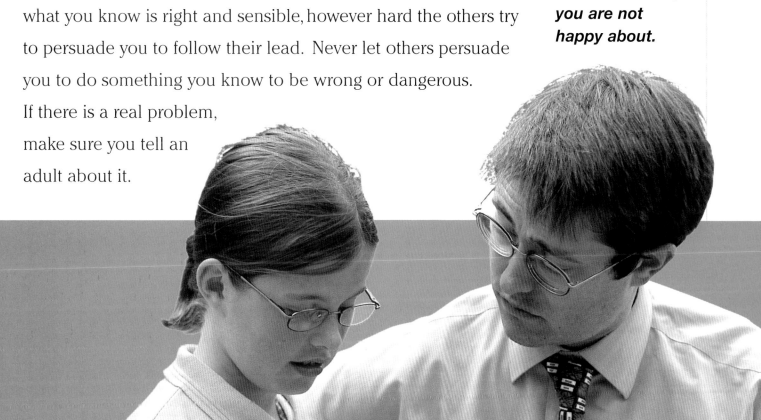

# How to handle arguments

Most people come into contact with other people at home, at school or work and in their spare time. It is impossible to agree with everybody else all the time and so there will be arguments and disagreements now and again. Some ways of handling these are good, but others just make matters worse.

▼ *After an argument, always try to apologize and make up.*

▶ *Arguing does not help to solve problems.*

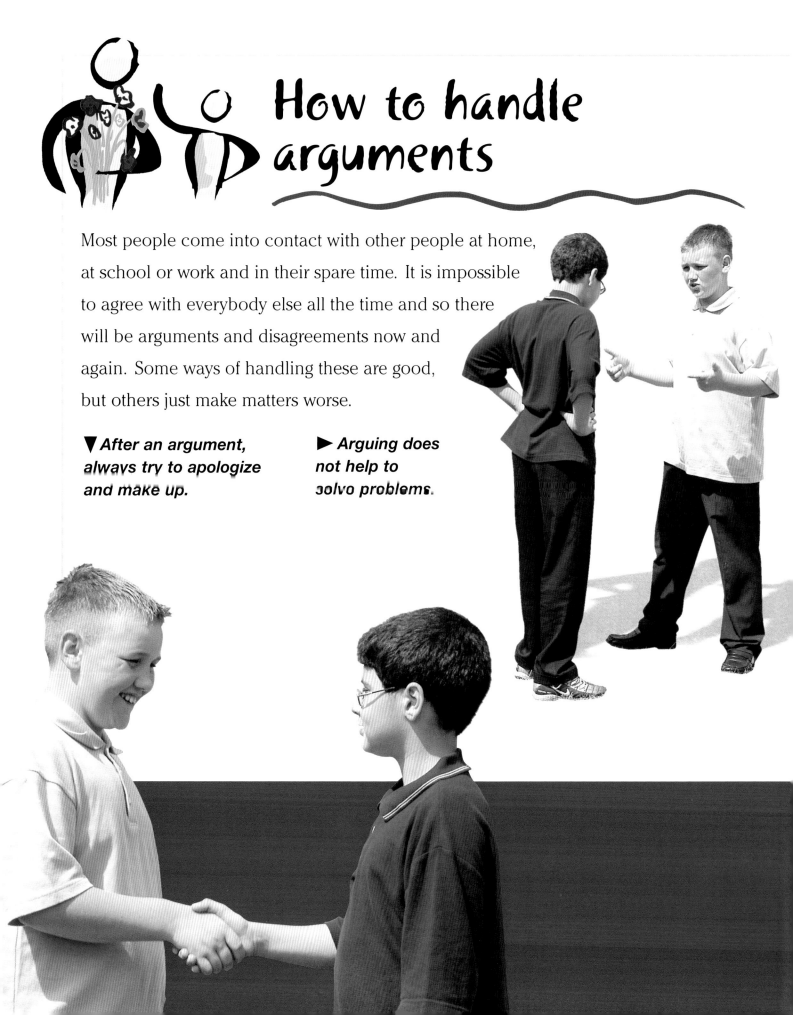

It is important that you let people know if there is something that you are not happy with. If you try to do this politely and without getting cross, they will respond more willingly and listen to you. Try to explain why you are not happy, and then listen carefully as you give them a chance to explain their point of view.

Try to avoid getting angry, losing your temper, shouting, slamming doors and sulking! These do not help to solve disagreements; the situation just gets worse as everybody gets more and more upset.

A compromise is a way of solving a problem. It means that both people have to give in a little bit, but both gain a little as well. For example, if you want to go to a friend's and stay overnight, but your parents are not happy with your plan, then a sensible compromise might be for you to go to your friend's but for your parents to collect you at bedtime.

▶ *Sulking can make problems worse rather than better.*

# ⌇⌇ Action Zone

To avoid getting angry, you often need to use some self-control. This is not always easy, especially if someone or something has really upset you! Try to do something else for a few seconds to let your anger calm a little before you act. Some people count to ten, others stand still and take five deep breaths. Can you think of something you could do that will take about ten seconds? Perhaps you could recite the names of your soccer team's players in your head, or say the alphabet backwards.

# Family change

Families do not stay the same forever. They change continuously as new babies are born, children grow into adults and have their own families, and elderly people die. Other family changes come about when adults make decisions about how they want to live and who they want to live with.

When two adults meet and fall in love, they often expect to live together for the rest of their lives. As the years pass, though, their feelings for each other may change and they may decide that they do not want to live together any more.

▲ *When a new baby is born, relationships in a family will change.*

▲ *It can be very distressing to hear adults arguing.*

This can be very distressing for any children who are involved. It is important for the children to understand that it is not their fault and that they are not to blame for what is happening to the family.

Sometimes, two families may join together. Two adults, each with children, may decide to live together. The children each gain a new parent and new brothers or sisters. They may all find it difficult to adjust at first, and everybody in the new family will need to try hard to be considerate and helpful to the others.

# Action Zone

Has your family changed recently? If it has, and you're happy, that's great! If you're unhappy, you need to talk. Think of an adult you really trust – it might be someone who is not directly involved, perhaps a teacher or another relative – and tell them how you feel. Listen to them too, there may be facts that you don't know about that affect what is happening to your family. Be patient as well, things that seem really bad now may improve given a little time.

▲ *Talking about your feelings often helps you to feel better.*

# When someone dies

We all know that living things die, but it is very sad and upsetting when someone who you are close to dies.

If somebody dies very suddenly, perhaps after a road accident, their family and friends may suffer from shock for a while afterwards. People react differently: some may want company and to talk about the person who has died, but others may want to be left alone so that they can grieve quietly in private.

▼ *You can share precious memories of someone who has died by looking at photographs of happy times you spent together.*

▲ *Putting flowers on a grave can help you to feel close to someone who has died.*

When someone dies after a long illness, their family and friends may be sad but the death will not be a shock to them. If the person had suffered a lot, or had been in a lot of pain, they may feel relieved that the suffering is over.

It usually helps to talk about the person who has died. You can feel close to them and relive memories of happy times you spent with them. Although you may be very sad, you will feel better as time passes.

# ⟨?⟩ Fantastic Facts

Different communities have different traditions and different ways of thinking about death. People may wear clothes of a special colour to show that they are 'in mourning' for someone who has died. In most Western countries, mourning clothes are black, but in other countries they may be white or yellow.

▲ *Muslim men pray together at a grave in China.*

# Growing up

As you get older, your attitudes and feelings will develop. Your relationships with friends and family will change as your interests and outlook change.

Many children feel, as they grow up, that they want to be more independent. Your safety is probably your parents' main concern, so before you can gain any independence you need to prove that you are reliable, honest and sensible. Your parents may then be able to allow you some additional independence. Your relationship with them will change a little as they begin to see you as a young adult rather than a child.

▶ *As you grow up, you may take up new hobbies and interests.*

The games you played and enjoyed may begin to seem childish as you grow up. Your interests may change, and so may the people you want to spend time with. This is fine, but try not to hurt an old friend's feelings by suddenly dropping them for somebody new.

Changes in feelings and relationships can lead to arguments and disagreements. Remember to control your anger as much as you can, and deal calmly with each situation that arises.

▶ *You may not be keen to play with a younger brother or sister, but try to think about how they are feeling too.*

## Action Zone

Here are some ideas for ways in which you can start to take responsibility for yourself and let your parents see that you are growing up:

● look after yourself: wash, clean your teeth, brush your hair etc. without being reminded

● look after your belongings: pack your own school bag, remember your own swimming kit, don't lose things

● look after your room: put clothes away, keep your books and toys tidy, help with the cleaning

● look after your family: offer to help a younger brother or sister, help clear up after a meal, help with the shopping.

If you can do all of these, you've made a good start!

▲ *Show how responsible you are by taking care of yourself.*

# Glossary

**argument** exchanging views - often angrily.

**attitude** the way you feel about something or someone.

**bullying** doing something that makes another person unhappy.

**communicate** to pass information to someone else.

**compromise** a solution that both parties are happy with.

**considerate** thinking about someone else and not just yourself.

**co-operate** help someone else.

**distress** causing someone to be upset.

**extended family** a familly unit made up of more than just a mother, father and children.

**independence** freedom to control your own actions.

**loyal** can be trusted.

**mourning clothes** traditional clothes worn to show respect for the dead.

**navigate** find the correct way.

**peer** a person of the same age.

**relationship** the way two or more people are linked together.

**reliable** is able to be trusted and relied on.

**responsibility** be in control of.

**rumour** a story that is spread about.

**selfish** no thought for other people's interests of feelings.

**sibling** a brother or sister.

**society** a community made up of lots of people.

**spiteful** to be unkind on purpose.

**tradition** something that has been done previously and is now an accepted way of doing things.

# Other books to read

*How do I feel about My Parents' Divorce* by J. Cole (Franklin Watts, 1999)

*How do I feel about Bullies and Gangs* by Julie Johnson (Franklin Watts, 1999)

*How do I feel about My Stepfamily* by Julie Johnson (Franklin Watts, 1999)

*How do I feel about Loneliness and Making Friends* by Sarah Levete (Franklin Watts, 1999)

*How do I feel about When People Die* by Sarah Levete (Franklin Watts, 1999)

*Let's talk about When a Parent Dies* by Elizabeth Weitzman (Heinemann Library, 1998)

*Let's talk about Your Parents' Divorce* by Elizabeth Weitzman (Heinemann Library, 1998)

## Useful addresses

NCH Action for Children
Tel: 020 7704 7000
Fax: 020 7226 2537

Childline
Tel: 0800 1111

Bullying Online is a charity which can deal with your queries via email
help@bullying.co.uk

Kidscape is a charity dedicated to preventing bullying and child sexual abuse.
Tel: 08451 205 204
E-mail feedback@kidscape.org.uk

Samaritans
Tel: 08457 90 90 90